Fun with Hieroglyphs

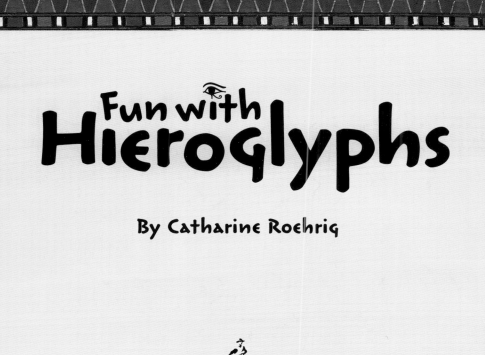

Fun with Hieroglyphs

By Catharine Roehrig

SIMON & SCHUSTER BOOKS FOR YOUNG READERS
THE METROPOLITAN MUSEUM OF ART
NEW YORK

THE METROPOLITAN MUSEUM OF ART
1000 Fifth Avenue, New York, NY 10028
212.570.3894   www.metmuseum.org

SIMON & SCHUSTER BOOKS FOR YOUNG READERS
is a trademark of Simon & Schuster, Inc.

Manufactured in China
10 9 8 7 6 5 4 3 2

Produced by the Department of Special Publications, The Metropolitan Museum of Art:
Robie Rogge, Publishing Manager; Jessica Schulte, Project Editor;
Atif Toor and Anna Raff, Designers; Gillian Moran, Production Associate.
All photography by The Metropolitan Museum of Art Photograph Studio unless otherwise noted.

ISBN 13: 978-1-58839-272-5 (The Metropolitan Museum of Art)
ISBN 10: 1-58839-272-4 (The Metropolitan Museum of Art)
ISBN 13: 978-1-4169-6114-7 (Simon & Schuster Books for Young Readers)
ISBN 10: 1-4169-6114-3 (Simon & Schuster Books for Young Readers)

Library of Congress Cataloging-in-Publication Data

Roehrig, Catharine H.
 Fun with hieroglyphs / by Catharine Roehrig. — 1st ed.
  p. cm.
 ISBN-13: 978-1-4169-6114-7
 ISBN-10: 1-4169-6114-3
 1. Egyptian language—Writing, Hieroglyphic—Juvenile literature.
 I. Metropolitan Museum of Art (New York, N.Y.) II. Title.

PJ1097.R64 2008
493'.111—dc22

2007044485

A previous version of this work was published in 1990
by The Metropolitan Museum of Art, New York, and Viking, a division of Penguin Books USA Inc.

Contents

Introduction

About 5,000 years ago, in the northeast corner of Africa, the people living along the Nile River began to set their language down in writing. Like most cultures that are just beginning to invent a writing system, the ancient Egyptians used pictures to write their language. Eventually the symbols came to represent sounds. The pictures became known as hieroglyphs, or "sacred inscriptions," because they were often written on the walls of temples.

The Egyptians continued to use hieroglyphic writing for more than 3,500 years, until about AD 400. After that, the language was written in the Greek alphabet with several extra letters

Journey to Abydos (detail). Egyptian, Dynasty 18 (ca.1550–1295 BC). Tempera on paper.

added for Egyptian sounds that did not exist in Greek. This late form of Egyptian is called Coptic. Eventually Coptic was replaced by Arabic, the language spoken in Egypt today. Since no one was left who knew how to read, or write, or speak the ancient language, it died out. Only hieroglyphs were left as clues that the language ever existed.

It was not until 1799 that the secret to deciphering hieroglyphs—the Rosetta Stone—was unearthed in Egypt. It took another twenty-three years before a young Frenchman, Jean François Champollion, decoded the writings on the stone and discovered what the hieroglyphs represented.

When you have finished reading this book, you (unlike travelers of long ago) will be able to recognize and pronounce many of the hieroglyphs that can be seen in Egyptian inscriptions. You will even be able to recognize the names of some of the pharaohs. The twenty-four hieroglyphic stamps in this kit represent sounds, and once you know them, you will be ready to stamp sentences using symbols from this ancient language.

Inner Coffin of Khonsu (detail). Egyptian (Thebes), Dynasty 19 (ca. 1279–1213 BC). Painted wood and gesso.

Mysterious Hieroglyphs

Before 1822, when the hieroglyphic code was broken, travelers to Egypt were intrigued by the mysterious symbols that they saw carved on the walls of temples and tombs. Since no one could tell them what the hieroglyphs meant, they made up fantastic translations. They thought that hieroglyphs recorded magical spells and secret religious practices.

The Hieroglyphic Alphabet

Nofretari Kneeling in Adoration (detail). Egyptian (Thebes), Dynasty 19 (ca.1295–1186 BC). Tempera on paper.

When you look at hieroglyphs on a statue, or a wall, or in a book, you may think that each hieroglyph stands for a word. In a few cases, you would be correct. Some hieroglyphs do mean what they represent. For example, the hieroglyph ●, a picture of the sun (usually shown as a circle with a dot in the middle), means *sun*.

However, hieroglyphic writing is more than picture writing. Although at first they probably were used as pictures, some hieroglyphs eventually began to represent sounds.

Twenty-four hieroglyphs represent the single sounds found in the Egyptian language. These hieroglyphs are used like the letters of the alphabet.

For example, the hieroglyph 🦉, an owl, stands for the sound *m*, not for the word *owl*. The hieroglyph 🥣, a basket, stands for the sound *k*, not for the word *basket*.

24 Single-Sound Hieroglyphs

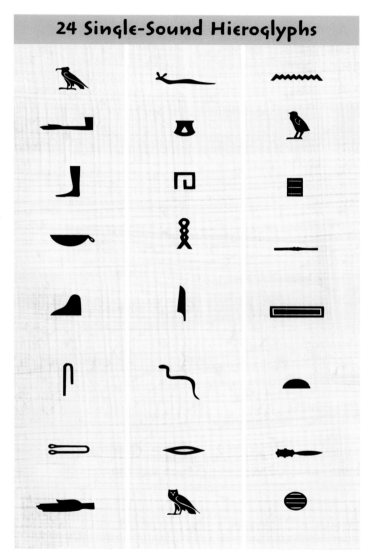

Stela of Aafenmut. Egyptian (Thebes), Dynasty 22 (ca. 924–889 BC). Painted wood.

Sound Bite

There are many words and ideas that cannot be shown in a simple picture. For example, how would you make a picture of the verb *to see*? You might draw a picture of an eye, but this could mean lots of things. It could mean *eye*, or *look*, or *see*. You could find another word that sounds like the word *see* and draw a picture of that. For example, you might choose the noun *sea*. But a picture of the sea might mean *ocean*, or *wave*, or *water*. A clearer way to write the verb *to see* would be to spell out the sounds with letters. Most of the hieroglyphs that appear in Egyptian writing are being used to spell out words.

Often, but not always, a hieroglyph and a letter represent the same sound. But since English and Egyptian are not from the same language family, some sounds used by the Egyptians do not exist in the alphabet. And some English sounds do not exist in Egyptian.

The Egyptians didn't hear a difference between the sounds *f* and *v*, so both are represented by the hieroglyph. The sound for this hieroglyph is *f*.

They also didn't hear a difference between the sounds *r* and *l*, so they are represented by the hieroglyph. The sound for this hieroglyph is *r*.

Unfamiliar Sounds

Hieroglyph	Non-English Sound	Closest English Sound
	like the Arabic letter ﻉ, 'ain; a sound made at the back of the throat	like **a** as in m**a**ke
	an emphatic **h**	like **h** as in h**ā**!
	guttural **ch**, found in the Scottish word lo**ch** or the Arabic letter ﺥ, hā. This sound is sometimes written **kh** in English.	k
	like the **ch** found in German	h
	like the Arabic letter ﻕ, ḳāf; a **k** sound made at the back of the throat	k

The Egyptians also had no sound for the English *th*. With this sound you have a choice. To be strictly accurate, spell out *th*, using the hieroglyphs for *t* and *h*. For example, the word *this* would be spelled:

t + h + i + s

Or you can use or to represent *th*. Neither hieroglyph represents a sound found in English, so you can pretend that they sound like *th*. Remember that *th* has two sounds in English. The first is the *th* sound heard in words like *this*, *the*, and o*th*er. The second is the *th* sound heard in words like *th*ree, *th*row, and bo*th*. Try saying these words until you can hear the difference.

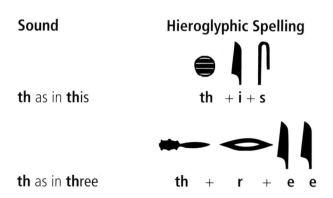

Sound	Hieroglyphic Spelling
th as in **this**	th + i + s
th as in **three**	th + r + e e

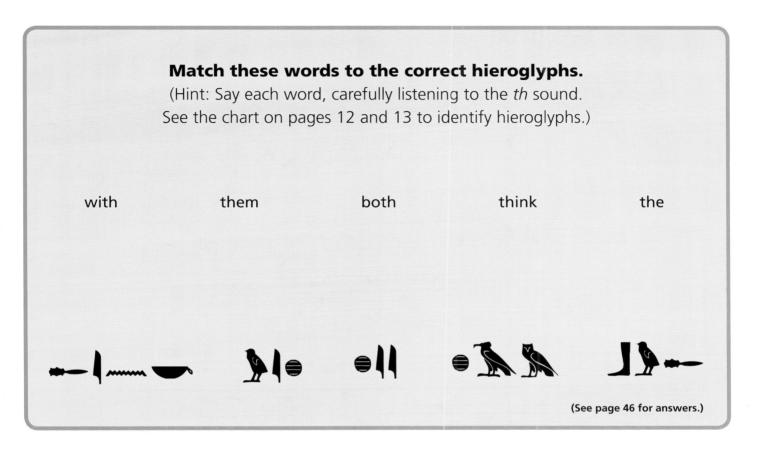

Match these words to the correct hieroglyphs.
(Hint: Say each word, carefully listening to the *th* sound.
See the chart on pages 12 and 13 to identify hieroglyphs.)

with   them   both   think   the

(See page 46 for answers.)

On the following pages is a list of letters and the sounds that they represent. Next to each letter you will find the hieroglyph that is closest to each letter's sound.

A few letters—most vowels and several consonants—have more than one sound, so these letters have more than one hieroglyph. Three letters (*c*, *h*, and *k*) have two hieroglyphs for one sound; for these, choose the hieroglyph that looks the best.

Remember, it is the *sound* that is important when writing with the hieroglyphic alphabet.

Letter	Hieroglyph	Sound
A	vulture	Use the vulture for the **a** sound in words like **a**t and b**a**t or **a**bout and **a**cross.
A	forearm	Use the forearm for the **a** sound in words like **a**ble and m**a**ke.
B	foot	Use the foot for the **b** sound in words like **b**all or **b**oy.
C	basket / hillside	Use either the basket or the hillside for the hard **c** sound in words like **c**amel, **c**andy, and s**ch**ool.
C	folded cloth	Use the folded cloth for the soft **c** sound in words like **c**ent and ni**c**e.
CH	hobble rope	Use the hobble rope for the **ch** sound in words like **ch**oose and **ch**ur**ch**.
D	hand	Use the hand for the **d** sound in words like **d**elta and **d**ime.
E	vulture	Use the vulture for the **e** sound in words like **e**arn and ov**e**r or b**e**t and **e**lf.
E	two reed leaves	Use two reed leaves for the **e** sound in words like r**ea**d and r**ee**d.

Letter	Hieroglyph	Sound
F	horned viper	Use the horned viper for the **f** sound in words like **f**ar and **f**ort and **ph**araoh.
G	pot stand	Use the pot stand for the hard **g** sound in words like **g**irl and **g**o.
H	shelter / rope	Use either the shelter or the rope for the **h** sound in words like be**h**ind, **h**it, and **wh**o.
I	one reed leaf	Use one reed leaf for both the short **i** sound in words like b**i**t and st**i**ll, and the long **i** sound in words like b**i**te and **i**vy.
J	cobra	Use the cobra for the **j** sound in words like **j**am and **j**inx or **G**eor**g**e and **g**entle.
K	basket / hillside	Use either the basket or the hillside for the **k** sound in words like ba**ck** and **k**eep.
L	open mouth	Use the open mouth for the **l** sound in words like **l**ate and **l**oaf.
M	owl	Use the owl for the **m** sound in words like cru**mb** and **m**ud.
N	water	Use the water for the **n** sound in words like bo**n**e and **N**ile.

Letter	Hieroglyph	Sound
O	vulture quail chick	Use the vulture for the **o** sound in words like c**o**t and **O**liver and b**ou**ght and t**ou**r. Use the quail chick for the **o** sound in words like h**oo**t and m**oo**n, b**oa**t and **o**pen, or f**oo**t and s**oo**t.
P	stool	Use the stool for the **p** sound in words like **p**et and **p**ond.
Q	basket + quail chick	Use the basket and the quail chick for the **qu** (**kw**) sound in words like **qu**een and **qu**ick.
R	open mouth	Use the open mouth for the **r** sound in words like c**r**own and **r**ain.
S	folded cloth door bolt	Use the folded cloth for the **s** sound in words like cat**s** or hou**s**e. Use the door bolt for the **s** sound in words like boy**s** and plea**s**e.
SH	lake	Use the lake for the **sh** sound in words like **sh**ip, ma**ch**ine, and **Sch**midt.
T	bread loaf	Use the bread loaf for the **t** sound in words like le**t** and **t**ell.

Letter	Hieroglyph	Sound
TH	cow's belly (unknown*)	Use the cow's belly for the **th** sound in words like bo**th** and **th**rough. Use this hieroglyph for the **th** sound in words like bo**th**er and **th**e.
U	quail chick one reed leaf + quail chick	Use the quail chick for the **u** sound in words like c**u**t and g**u**ll or f**u**ll and p**u**ll. Use one reed leaf and the quail chick for the **u** sound in words like m**u**le and f**ue**l.
V	horned viper	Use the horned viper for the **v** sound in words like co**v**er and **v**ideo.
W	quail chick	Use the quail chick for the **w** sound in words like co**w**, **w**hat, **w**here, and **w**ind.
X	basket + folded cloth	Use the basket and the folded cloth for the **x** sound in words like bo**x**, e**x**tra, and soc**ks**.
Y	one reed leaf two reed leaves	Use one reed leaf for the **y** sound in words like cra**y**on, **y**es, and **y**ou. Use two reed leaves for the **y** sound in words like Mar**y** and **Y**vonne.
Z	door bolt	Use the door bolt for the **z** sound in words like **z**ebra and **x**ylophone.

*This hieroglyph's meaning is still unknown.

Some letters in the alphabet sound like others, so pay attention to the way a letter sounds when you're choosing a hieroglyph. For example, in the word *cat*, the *c* sounds like *k*, and in the word *cent*, the *c* sounds like *s*. These letters use the same hieroglyph because they share the same sound.

Similar Sounds

Letter	Hieroglyph	Sound
c		**k** as in **c**at
c		**s** as in **c**ent
qu		**kw** as in **qu**it
x		**ks** as in bo**x**
x		**z** as in **x**ylophone

Stamp these words in hieroglyphs.

at	boot	chin	map
cat	twin	wax	tree
to	kiss	zip	sugar
food	gym	clue	

(See page 46 for answers.)

Cat. Egyptian, Ptolemaic period (ca. 330–30 BC). Bronze.

Match these words to the correct hieroglyphs.

(Hint: Pay attention to the sound, not the spelling.)

judge

queen

neighbor

weather

xerox

enough

sphinx

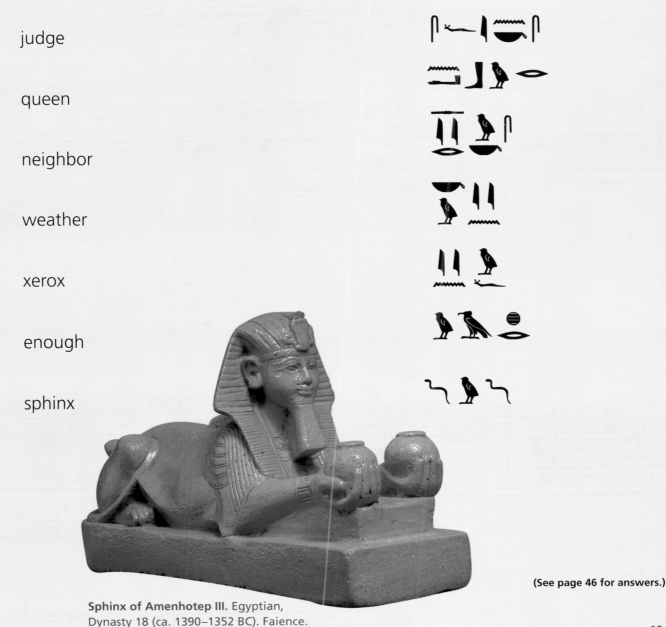

Sphinx of Amenhotep III. Egyptian,
Dynasty 18 (ca. 1390–1352 BC). Faience.

(See page 46 for answers.)

The Orientation of Hieroglyphs

Unlike the letters in the alphabet, hieroglyphs can be read in more than one direction. They can be read from left to right like English, or from right to left like Arabic and Hebrew, or in columns from top to bottom like Chinese.

FROM LEFT TO RIGHT
FROM RIGHT TO LEFT
DOWN

You can tell which way hieroglyphs are supposed to be read by looking at the animals, plants, and people. If they face left, start reading from the left. If they face right, begin at the right. In other words, read toward the faces. Almost always the hieroglyphs that refer to a person face the same direction as the person.

Stela of Ptahmose (detail). Egyptian, Dynasty 19 (ca. 1295–1186 BC). Limestone.

The direction in which a hieroglyphic text was written depended on the kind of text it was and how it was used. When the Egyptians wrote long inscriptions (official documents, for example, or long historical texts without illustrations), they usually wrote the hieroglyphs facing right. The inscription would be read from right to left, the opposite of how English is read. However, if an inscription was used to decorate a building, the Egyptians often wrote the hieroglyphs in different directions.

When a hieroglyphic text is part of a scene that contains more than one person, the direction that the hieroglyphs face tells which words refer to which person. On the stone slab or stela at left, a man with upraised arms is making an offering to the god Osiris, ruler of the afterworld. The two short columns of text near Osiris give Osiris's name and titles. Like Osiris, they face right. The six columns of text at the right give the titles of the man and record his offering to the god. Like the man, these hieroglyphs face left.

Stela of the Chancellor Neferiu (detail). Egyptian, Dynasty 9 (ca. 2100–2090 BC). Painted limestone.

Left to Right, Right to Left

On the stela above, there is a niche (the indented rectangular area in the center), which represents a door. The hieroglyphs and people on either side of the door face it in a symmetrical fashion. Look carefully at the hieroglyphs of animals, plants, and people. The ones on the left face right, so you would read toward the left. Those on the right face left so you would read toward the right.

Write Like an Egyptian

Since fifteen of the hieroglyphic stamps in this kit face left, you can use them to write words only from left to right or from top to bottom. If you want to write from right to left, like the Egyptians often did, you must draw these fifteen hieroglyphs yourself. Here they are, facing right. Practice first by tracing the hieroglyphs, then try drawing them freehand. The other nine hieroglyphic stamps are symmetrical and can be used in either direction.

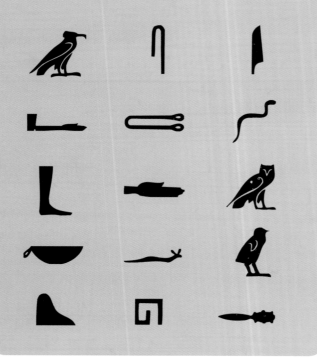

When the Egyptians wrote a word in hieroglyphs, they didn't just write one hieroglyph after another. They arranged them carefully, making them look attractive. For example, if an Egyptian had wanted to write the name *Frank* in hieroglyphs, he wouldn't have written it like this:

F   R   A   N   K

He probably would have artfully arranged the hieroglyphs and written them like this:

F   N
R   A   K

Grouping the hieroglyphs this way would not only fit the space better but also would look more attractive to an Egyptian. As you stamp messages and as you read the ones that you receive from your friends, remember that hieroglyphic words can be written horizontally (from left to right and from right to left) as well as vertically (from top to bottom). If one hieroglyph is above another, always read the one on top first.

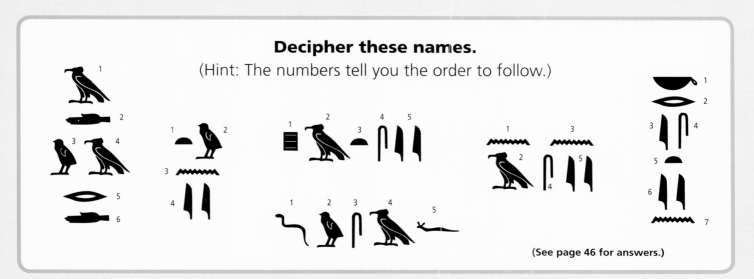
The Cartouche

When a new pharaoh came to the throne in Egypt, he took a coronation name. Both the coronation name and the personal name of the pharaoh were written inside a special frame called a cartouche, an oval with a line at the bottom. This actually represents a section of rope that is tied together at one end, forming a loop.

In this wall painting, King Haremhab stands facing the goddess Isis. Above his head are the cartouches recording his names. The highlighted cartouche is an expanded version of his personal name, "Haremhab, Beloved of Amun." Kings' names were often not spelled alphabetically, but Egyptians would understand what each hieroglyph represented. Notice that the hieroglyphs face left, just like Haremhab.

Haremhab Before Isis (detail). Egyptian (Thebes), Dynasty 18 (ca. 1323–1295 BC). Tempera on paper.

Now try stamping your own name both horizontally and vertically. First, decide which hieroglyphs to use by listening to the sound of your name. For example, Susan is pronounced SOOZIN so you might use these hieroglyphs:

Decide how the hieroglyphs you have chosen will look best together. SOOZIN can be written several other ways:

Like the Egyptians, you can leave out unimportant vowels if you like. Here the *I* is left out of SOOZIN:

If your name is long, you can shorten it. ALEXANDER becomes ALXANDR:

CHRISTOPHER becomes KRISTOFR:

Find the hieroglyphic words.

In the puzzle, hunt for the words listed below. When you find a word, circle it. You can go left to right, top to bottom, or diagonally. One word (*man*) has been found for you. Can you find the items listed in this wall painting of a fishing expedition?

Menna and His Family Fishing and Fowling (detail). Egyptian (Thebes), Dynasty 18 (ca. 1550--1295 BC). Tempera on paper.

man

bird

fish

cat

crocodile

lily

goose

eggs

river

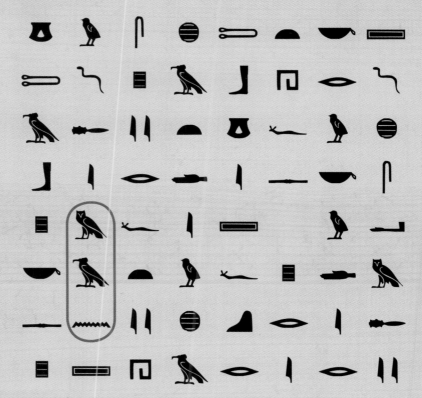

(See page 46 for answers.)

Stamping Secret Messages

Prince and His Father, King Ramesses III, Before Hat-Hor. Egyptian (Thebes), Dynasty 20 (ca. 1195–1080 BC). Tempera on paper.

Now that you know all about the twenty-four alphabetic hieroglyphs and their sounds and how hieroglyphs are read, you are all set to begin writing letters and other secret messages to your friends using the stamps in this kit.

Make sure to give your friends a decoding sheet with the hieroglyphs and their sounds so that they, like you, can decipher these ancient symbols. You can make a sheet by stamping the hieroglyphs and writing the sound(s) that they represent by each one. Or instead, you can photocopy the "Letters, Hieroglyphs, and Their Sounds" chart on pages 12 and 13.

On the opposite page are words and phrases that you might want to use in your messages. As a scribe might write:

H A P Y   R I T N G

Hieroglyphic Words and Phrases

Yes	No	Help	Okay	Kiss	Hello
Surprise	Private	Keep Out		No Trespassing	
Top Secret		Urgent		Confidential	
Thank You		Happy New Year		Happy Father's Day	
I Miss You		Get Well		Happy Mother's Day	
Good Luck		Thinking of You		Happy Birthday	
Congratulations		Come to a Party		Happy Valentine's Day	

Counting with Hieroglyphs

Like members of every other culture, Egyptians needed to count. They needed numbers to measure their fields, take inventories, calculate taxes, and build temples, tombs, and houses. Just like ours, their counting system was based on the number 10. But instead of using a different symbol for each number from 1 through 9, the Egyptians had one hieroglyph for 1, one for 10, and so on.

The numbers most often found in Egyptian texts are I which stands for 1, ∩ which stands for 10, and I which stands for 1,000.

A hieroglyph is repeated as many times as necessary to show the numbers from 1 through 9, the tens from 10 through 90, and so on.

The number 7 would be written like this:

I I I I
I I I

The number 25 would be written this way:

∩ I I I
  I I

The number 143 would be:

ℓ ∩ ∩ I I
  ∩ ∩ I

The number 1066 would be written:

I ∩ ∩ ∩ I I I
  ∩ ∩ ∩ I I I

Number	Hieroglyph
1	I \ stroke
10	∩ \ cattle hobble
100	ℓ \ coil of rope
1,000	I \ lotus plant
10,000	I \ finger
100,000	tadpole
1,000,000	god with arms supporting the sky

More Than Enough

The Egyptians wanted to be certain that they would have enough of every necessity after they died, so offering texts were written. These texts contained information about what they needed most in the afterlife. These items included bread, beer, the meat of cattle and birds, cloth, and stone jars for oils and perfumes. To be certain that they would not run out of anything, they wrote the number ⚊ or 1,000 in front of each offering.

In the stela at right, the nobleman Mechechi is seated before a table filled with offerings. (The hieroglyphs ▮☰🦉 on the top row of the stela spell his name.) Around the table are the standard items that each spirit needs in the afterlife. On top of the table are hieroglyphs that look like feathers, but they are really loaves of bread that have been cut in half. Beside the table are more bread and beer. Above the table are cattle, fowl, alabaster, and linen cloth. Mechechi asks to receive 1,000 of each as indicated by the ⚊ to the right of each object.

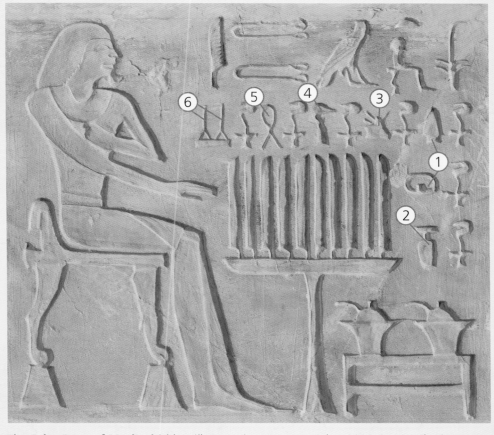

The False Door of Mechechi (detail). Egyptian, Dynasty 6 (ca. 2323–2150 BC). Limestone.

①bread ②beer ③cattle ④fowl ⑤alabaster ⑥linen cloth

Stela of Montuwoser (detail). Egyptian, Dynasty 12 (ca.1961–1917 BC). Painted limestone.

In the above detail of a stela, hieroglyphs record a date at the beginning of the row. (Remember to start on the far right—the direction that the birds face.) The first two hieroglyphs of the date, the tall one and the round one, stand for the word *year* and are followed by a number. Dates were recorded differently back then. Egyptians started counting years at 1 each time a new ruler came to the throne.

This text was written in year ∩¹¹¹¹¹ or 17 of King Kheper-ka-Re's reign. In the cartouche on the left of the line is the king's name, Kheper-ka-Re or "may he live forever." Of course, kings did not live or rule forever. Few pharaohs reigned for more than ∩ or 20 or ∩∩ or 30 years, and many ruled for fewer than ∩¹¹¹¹ or 15 years.

Write these hieroglyphs as numerals.

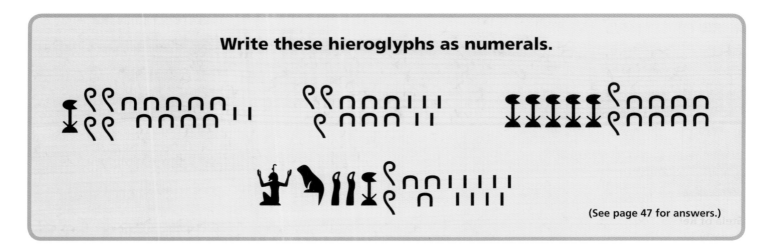

(See page 47 for answers.)

The longest reign of an Egyptian pharaoh is almost unbelievable. It was recorded for Pepi II, who lived at the end of the Old Kingdom, more than 𓏭𓏭𓏭𓏭 or 4,000 years ago. Pepi ruled for at least 𓆓𓆓𓆓𓆓𓆓‖ or 94 years, the longest recorded reign of any ruler in the world. Since he was at least ‖‖‖ or 6 when he became king, Pepi must have reached the age of 𓆼 or 100 before he died.

In the stela below, there are offerings of cattle, fowl, alabaster, and cloth. The lotus beneath each hieroglyph tells how much of each item is being offered.

Stela of Rehuerdjersen (detail). Egyptian (Abydos), Dynasty 12 (ca. 1981–1952 BC). Limestone.

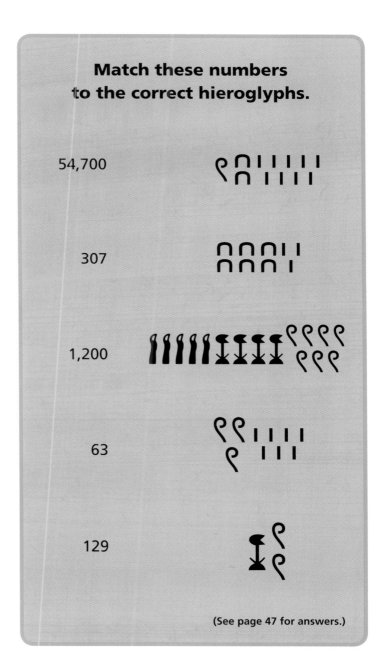

Match these numbers to the correct hieroglyphs.

54,700

307

1,200

63

129

(See page 47 for answers.)

Hieroglyphic Clues

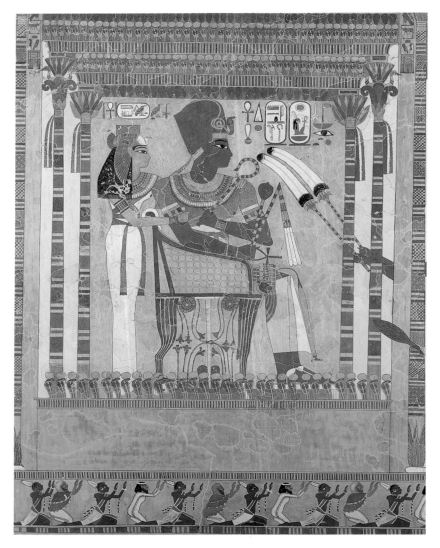

Amenhotep III and His Mother, Mutemua, in a Kiosk. Egyptian (Thebes), Dynasty 18 (ca. 1390–1352 BC). Tempera on paper.

When an Egyptian scribe wrote a word, he often left out the vowels and wrote just the consonants. But how can you tell the difference between the words *sun* and *son* if they are both spelled *sn*?

The Egyptians solved this problem by devising a way to indicate the meaning of a word or, at least, to give the reader a clue to its meaning. They used what we call determinatives, or hieroglyphs written at the end of a word, to indicate its general meaning. For example, the hieroglyph ⊗, a village with crossroads, would be written after the name of a town or even a country. In the same way, the name of a woman was identified with the hieroglyph 𓁐, and the name of a man with the hieroglyph 𓀀.

One other determinative, a single stroke, **I**, is very common. It tells you to read a hieroglyph as a picture. For example, the forearm ▬ usually represents the *a* sound, but written with a stroke, ⊤ means *arm*.

Determinatives have no sound; they just give a visual clue to the meaning of the word. For example:

gs 🦆 = goose   gs 🦆 I I I =geese   gs 🦆 👤 = Gus

RD THS!

Can you imagine how hard it would be to read if we left out the vowels? Write a short sentence leaving out the vowels and see if anyone else can understand it. Even you may not be able to read it after a few minutes.

A Scribe (detail). Egyptian (Thebes), Dynasty 18 (ca. 1550–1295 BC). Tempera on paper.

Hieroglyphic Determinatives

Hieroglyph	Meaning
seated man	man's name, male
seated woman	woman's name, female
seated man with hand to mouth	eat, drink, speak
village with crossroads	town or country name
sun	sun, light, time
house plan	house, building
water	water, liquid
walking legs	walk, run, go
papyrus roll	write, book, abstract idea
pintail duck	goose, duck, bird
three strokes	plural
eye	see

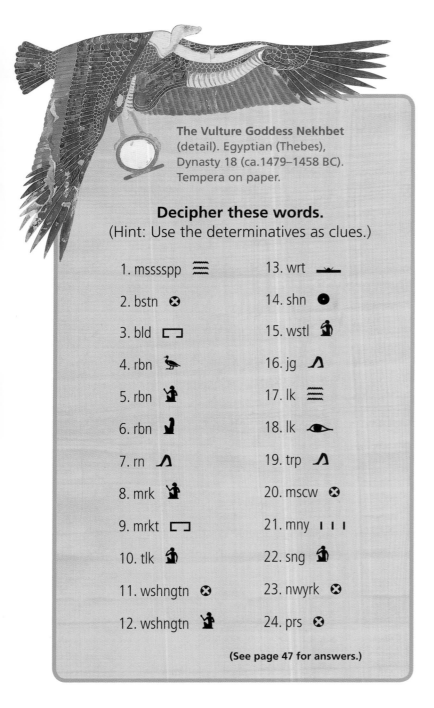

The Vulture Goddess Nekhbet (detail). Egyptian (Thebes), Dynasty 18 (ca.1479–1458 BC). Tempera on paper.

Decipher these words.
(Hint: Use the determinatives as clues.)

1. msssspp
2. bstn
3. bld
4. rbn
5. rbn
6. rbn
7. rn
8. mrk
9. mrkt
10. tlk
11. wshngtn
12. wshngtn
13. wrt
14. shn
15. wstl
16. jg
17. lk
18. lk
19. trp
20. mscw
21. mny
22. sng
23. nwyrk
24. prs

(See page 47 for answers.)

Now you can recognize the alphabetic hieroglyphs and some determinatives. But it is probably obvious that there are a lot of hieroglyphs that you don't recognize. More than 6,000 hieroglyphs have been identified. Luckily for scribes, only about 700 hieroglyphs were used at any one time. Only about 250 of these were used frequently.

Some of these hieroglyphs represent two sounds and are called biliterals (*bi* means *two*). Others represent three sounds and are called triliterals (*tri* means *three*). For example, the basket without a handle is a biliteral representing the sounds *n* and *b*, or *neb*. (The vowel is added so we can pronounce the sound.) The sign, showing a heart and a windpipe, is a triliteral and represents the sounds *n*, *f*, and *r*, or *nefer*. There are some others in the chart at right.

Sometimes biliterals are used alone to represent entire words. Sometimes they are combined with other hieroglyphs. For example, *sa* means *son* but *sat* means *daughter*. *per* means *house*. But ⬚ 𐤀 *peri* means *to go*. Three other Egyptian words you will see frequently are ⬭ *neb* meaning *lord* or *every*, ⊔ *ka* meaning *spirit*, and ↯ *nesut* meaning *king*.

Triliterals are also used alone or with other hieroglyphs to spell words. Some of these are surprising. Who could think that a heart and a windpipe ⬩ (pronounced *nefer*) could mean *beautiful*? Or that a beetle 🪲 (pronounced *kheper*) could mean *to come into existence*?

In spite of the economy of biliterals and triliterals, Egyptians often repeated sounds, using more hieroglyphs than they needed to spell a word. For example, the word *ankh*, meaning *life*, could be spelled either ☥ or ☥ 〰⬤, repeating the *n* and *kh*. The word *hotep*, meaning *offering*, could be written ⬥ or ⬥▪, repeating the *t* and *p*. With such a complicated system of spelling, it's no wonder that modern scholars needed many years to figure out how to decipher hieroglyphs!

Biliterals and Triliterals

Hieroglyph	Sound	Pronunciation
duck	s + a	sa
upraised arms	k + a	ka
house plan	p + r	per
beetle	kh + p + r	kheper
sandal strap	a + n + kh	ankh
table with bread	h + t + p	hotep
plant	s + u	soo

Magical Hieroglyphs

Amentet, Goddess of the West (detail). Egyptian, Dynasty 25 (ca. 712–664 BC). Painted wood panel.

A lthough hieroglyphs represent sounds and sometimes whole words, the Egyptians never forgot that they were also pictures of animals, plants, and other real things. At certain periods in Egyptian history, scribes seem to have treated the animal hieroglyphs as though they could magically come alive.

In some places, they left the legs off birds, perhaps so they wouldn't run away. For example, the vulture, the owl, and the quail chick would have looked like this:

In other places, scribes seem to have tried to "kill" dangerous animals so that these animals wouldn't harm a person in the afterlife. For example, the head was sometimes cut off of a poisonous horned viper, as in the detail from a coffin shown below. In other places, the cobra was similarly made harmless.

Coffin of Menqabu (detail). Egyptian, First Intermediate Period (2100–2061 BC). Painted wood.

Sacred Eye of Horus. Egyptian, Dynasty 18 (ca. 1390–1295 BC). Faience.

The Egyptians also used some hieroglyphs as amulets, or good luck charms, the way we might use a rabbit's foot today. For example, 👁, the *wedjat*-eye or the "eye of Horus," is a charm for healing that appears frequently in Egyptian art and jewelry. The god Horus is usually depicted as a man with a falcon's head. The lines that you see coming down from the wedjat-eye are the markings on a falcon's face. According to one Egyptian myth, Horus lost

Look Out

The two eyes of Horus were painted on the left side of many rectangular coffins, as shown on the coffin below. During the period when this type of coffin was built, the body was placed on its left side in the coffin. It's possible that the Egyptians believed that the dead person could see out of the eyes painted on the coffin.

Coffin of Khnum-nakht. Egyptian (possibly Asyut), Dynasty 12 (ca.1981–1802 BC). Painted wood.

one of his eyes in a great battle. The pieces of the eye were found by the god Thoth (usually shown as a man with the head of a bird called an ibis, as depicted at left), who magically put them back together, making the eye whole. The word *wedjat* means "to be whole" and the meaning gives the hieroglyph its healing power.

Another common Egyptian amulet is the scarab beetle 🪲. These little creatures are also called dung beetles because they collect huge balls of manure when they lay their eggs. The Egyptians frequently would have seen these tiny beetles pushing gigantic balls of dung in front of them across the ground. In Egyptian mythology, it was a scarab beetle that pushed the sun into the sky when it rose at dawn.

The beetle hieroglyph also represented sounds that could spell the Egyptian words that mean "come into existence" (the way the sun

Thoth (detail). Egyptian (probably Meir), Roman period (ca. AD 60–70). Painted plaster.

Scarab. Egyptian (Thebes), Dynasty 18 (ca. 1550–1295 BC). Steatite.

seems to come into existence each day when it rises). Probably because of the meaning of the hieroglyph, a single scarab was a very powerful amulet, and hundreds of thousands (or even millions) of scarabs were made by the ancient Egyptians.

Another Egyptian hieroglyph that may be familiar is ☥, the ankh. *Ankh* means "life." The hieroglyph often appears in scenes on temple walls and royal tombs where a god offers life to a king.

In the scene at right, the god Horus symbolically gives life to the king, who is represented here by a falcon.

Horus Offering an Ankh (detail). Egyptian (Lisht), Dynasty 12 (ca. 1981–1952 BC). Limestone.

The Egyptian Scribe

Many people take for granted the skills of reading and writing. But until perhaps one hundred years ago, the vast majority of people didn't have these skills. Even today, there are large numbers of people in some parts of the world who will never learn to read and write.

In the ancient world, very few people knew how to read and write. It wasn't considered necessary. Most people didn't learn from books. Rather, Egyptians learned everything that they needed to know from their parents or from the elders in their towns and villages. They could not read the hieroglyphic texts on the walls of a temple any more than you can.

In Egypt, reading and writing were skills of the trade or profession learned by a scribe. This profession was often passed along in families

Recording a Harvest (detail). Egyptian (Thebes), Dynasty 18 (ca.1550–1295 BC). Tempera on paper.

so that a person whose father was a scribe also became a scribe. This was true of most occupations, including agriculture, carpentry, and masonry. But sometimes a child who showed talent and a great interest would also be taught to read and write. Many scribes worked in the government and became very important people.

Each scribe usually owned a palette made of wood, like the one below. At one end are a cake of red paint and a cake of black paint. In the center is a long compartment with a sliding top that could be used to store brushes. The brush that the scribe used was made from a reed and frayed at one end. The scribe would wet this brush, then rub it on a dry cake of red or black paint.

Scribe's Palette and Brushes. Egyptian (Thebes), Dynasty 21 (ca. 1070–945 BC). Wood, ink, and reed.

Writer at Work

This small statuette shows a seated scribe with a scroll of papyrus. His kilt is drawn tightly around his knees to create a flat surface on which to write. He would have held a reed brush in his right hand and would have unrolled the papyrus with his left hand. The deep wrinkles across his chest indicate that he is no longer a young man.

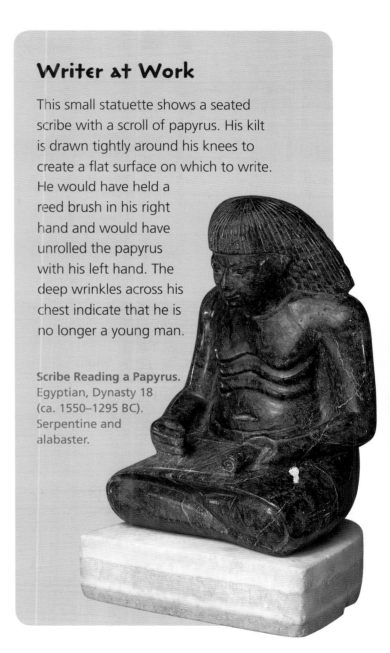

Scribe Reading a Papyrus. Egyptian, Dynasty 18 (ca. 1550–1295 BC). Serpentine and alabaster.

Coffin of Khnum-nakht (detail). Egyptian (possibly Asyut), Dynasty 12 (ca. 1981–1802 BC). Painted wood.

A young scribe learned his trade by copying texts. The texts that he copied were sometimes stories, sometimes poems, and sometimes lists of instructions on how to live an upright life. Much of the Egyptian literature that has been preserved comes from copies made by apprentice scribes. Some of these copies are incomplete, with the beginning, middle, or end missing. Others have mistakes in grammar and spelling.

When scribes were practicing their writing, they used inexpensive materials to write on instead of papyrus, a kind of paper that took a lot of time and a great deal of effort to make. For example, a scribe could use a piece of broken pottery or a smooth chip of limestone to practice writing. The sketch shown below was probably made by an artist decorating a royal tomb. The grid lines were made so that the draftsman could exactly copy the hieroglyphs from the sketch to the tomb wall, just as we use graph paper today to transfer drawings to larger surfaces.

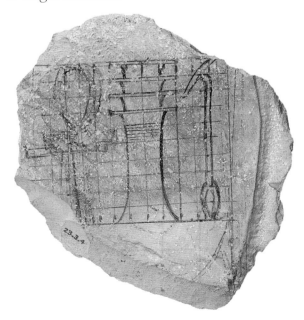

Artist's Gridded Sketch. Egyptian (Thebes), Dynasty 18 (ca. 1550–1295 BC). Inked limestone.

The Sign for Scribe

The hieroglyph for the word *scribe* is made up of a small palette, a water pot, and a reed brush. The same hieroglyph was used for the verb *to write*. You can tell the difference by looking at the determinative at the end of each word.

Scribe ends with a seated man.

To write ends with a roll of papyrus tied with a string.

The wooden copy board was another inexpensive writing surface. The board was covered with whitewash and used by the scribe. Later the surface could be scraped off or covered with a new coat of whitewash and used again. The scribe who wrote on the board at right copied parts of some funerary texts. Although his hieroglyphs are fairly easy to identify, the sizes are uneven and the spacing is awkward, suggesting that this scribe was not very experienced yet.

Scribe's Writing Board. Egyptian (vicinity of Akhim), Dynasty 11 (ca. 2124–1981 BC). Wood and gesso.

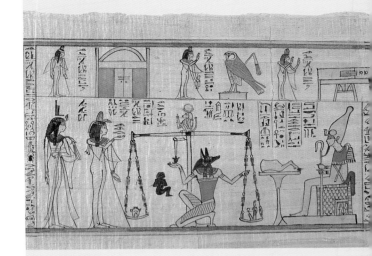

Nany's Funerary Papyri (detail). Egyptian (Thebes), Dynasty 21 (ca. 1070–945 BC). Inked papyrus.

Egyptian Paper

The papyrus plant once flourished along the banks of the Nile River and could grow to thirteen feet. In order to make paper, the outer layer of the papyrus's triangular-shaped stem was peeled away. Then the inner spongy layer was sliced into strips. Two layers of strips—one horizontal and one vertical—were laid on top of each other and weighted. When the sticky fluid from the plant bonded the strips into sheets, the sheets could be used as paper.

Two Styles of Writing

When we learn to write, we are taught two forms of writing. First we learn to print, making each letter with care. Then we are taught to run the letters of a word together in what is called cursive. It is much faster to write in cursive than to print, but since each person's handwriting is different, cursive can be hard to read.

The same is true of Egyptian writing. Egyptian scribes didn't always write in carefully formed hieroglyphs. Hieroglyphic writing was usually used on religious or official monuments. The texts carved on the walls of temples or painted in tombs are almost always written in hieroglyphs. Everything was written by hand, and each hieroglyph was drawn or carved separately. Remember, Egyptian scribes didn't have computers, scanners, printers, photocopiers, or stamps. Even a very good, quick scribe spent a lot of time copying a long hieroglyphic text.

When a scribe wrote something quickly or wrote less formal documents, such as tax records or receipts, he would use hieratic, which is like cursive. This was a much faster way to write, but it is harder for us to read because each person

All in the Details

Some hieroglyphs on temple walls and tombs are so carefully made that you can see the individual feathers on birds and veins on reed leaves.

Outer Coffin of Nephthys (detail). Egyptian, Dynasty 12 (ca. 1981–1802 BC). Painted wood.

wrote slightly differently. It is possible, however, to recognize individual hieroglyphs in hieratic writing.

The letter in hieratic at near right was written by a scribe for a man named Heqa-nakht. It mentions the amounts of grain that he expects to receive from his tenant farmers. (The Egyptians did not use money. Instead they paid with food, or cloth, or wine.) At first glance, the hieratic probably looks like meaningless scribbles. But examine it carefully and you will see that many of the scribbles resemble hieroglyphs. Compare the letter to the same one written in hieroglyphs by a modern Egyptologist. In the hieratic letter, see if you can find the hieratic 𓄿, an owl, and the hieratic 𓅂, a quail chick.

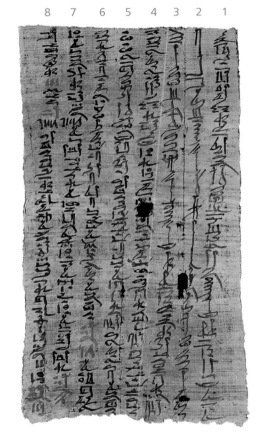

Letter for Heqa-nakht, Papyrus III.
Egyptian (Thebes), Dynasty 12
(ca. 1981–1802 BC). Papyrus.

An Egyptologist's transcription of
Letter for Heqa-nakht, Papyrus III.

41

Deciphering Hieroglyphs

Djehuty and His Mother Receiving Offerings (detail). Egyptian (Thebes), Dynasty 18 (ca. 1427–1400 BC). Tempera on paper.

The most recently written hieroglyphic text that has been found was written in AD 394. That's more than 1,600 years ago. At that time, only a few people still knew how to use this ancient writing system, and when they died, the skills to read and write hieroglyphs died with them.

Off and on for hundreds of years, people who saw the ancient hieroglyphic texts on gigantic statues or temple walls failed to decipher the writing. They failed partly because they didn't understand that most of the animals and plants that they saw represented sounds and spelled out words. They thought that each hieroglyph could be read as a word or as an idea. The early "translations" of hieroglyphic texts were often very imaginative, but totally incorrect.

The most important key to deciphering hieroglyphs was accidentally discovered in 1799 by a group of Frenchmen who had gone to Egypt with the invading army of Napoléon Bonaparte. While these men were preparing to build a fortress at the town known then as Rosetta, they uncovered a broken stela that was covered with writing. This stela, which can be dated precisely to March 27, 196 BC, is called the Rosetta Stone. It is probably the most famous Egyptian inscription ever found. It is certainly the most important. Why does this battered-looking piece of stone have so much value? It isn't a great work of art. The stone, basalt, isn't considered precious. The decree written on the stela is less important than many others. Rather, the value is in the writing itself: The decree has been written in more than one language.

The stone is split into three distinct sections. The top section is written in hieroglyphs, which were still used at the time to write official documents and religious texts. The middle is written in a script called demotic. This script represents a late form of the Egyptian language that was spoken at the time. The bottom section is written in ancient Greek because there were many Greeks living in Egypt in 196 BC, and most of them probably couldn't read hieroglyphs or demotic. (The Ptolemies, who ruled Egypt at this time, had come from Greece with Alexander the Great, who conquered the country in 332 BC. Although at the time they had ruled Egypt for more than one hundred years, the Ptolemies had not given up their Greek heritage or language.)

Hieroglyphic Writing

Demotic Writing

Greek Writing

Rosetta Stone. Egyptian (el-Rashid), 196 BC. Basalt.

Relief of Nebhepetre Mentuhotep II (detail). Egyptian (Thebes), Dynasty 11 (ca. 2051–2000 BC). Painted limestone.

In 1799, no one could read hieroglyphs or demotic, but ancient Greek was taught in schools, and it was possible to translate the Greek inscription on the Rosetta Stone. More importantly, it was possible for scholars to find the names of people and places in the Greek text, and then compare them to the same names in the Egyptian text.

Unfortunately, the earliest scholars still thought that hieroglyphs were a form of picture writing, with each symbol representing an entire word or idea. It wasn't until 1814 that an Englishman named Thomas Young realized that many hieroglyphs represented sounds and that a group of hieroglyphs could be used to spell a word. In most cases, Young could not understand the words, or even be certain of the sounds represented by the hieroglyphs, but he was on the right track. Young also proved that the hieroglyphs in a cartouche represented the name of a pharaoh.

For more than twenty years after the discovery of the Rosetta Stone, many people tried to decipher the texts. The man who finally succeeded was

Coptic Manuscript. Egyptian (Wadi an-Natrun), Coptic period (AD 200–1199). Inked paper.

Lots of Languages

As a child, Champollion had become interested in Egypt and was determined to decipher hieroglyphs. In preparation for this, he learned many languages, including Coptic, Arabic, and Hebrew, all of which (especially Coptic) have some relationship to ancient Egyptian.

a brilliant young Frenchman named Jean-François Champollion. Gradually, Champollion discovered which hieroglyphs represented which sounds. He learned that twenty-four hieroglyphs were alphabetic, standing for the single sounds that are included on the stamps. The others represented groups of sounds or were used as determinatives. (Thomas Young had suggested that there were different kinds of hieroglyphs, but he never got as far as Champollion in identifying them.) In 1822, at the age of thirty-one, Champollion became the first modern person who could actually decipher hieroglyphic writing. This made him the first person in almost 1,500 years who could read what the Egyptians had written about themselves and their culture.

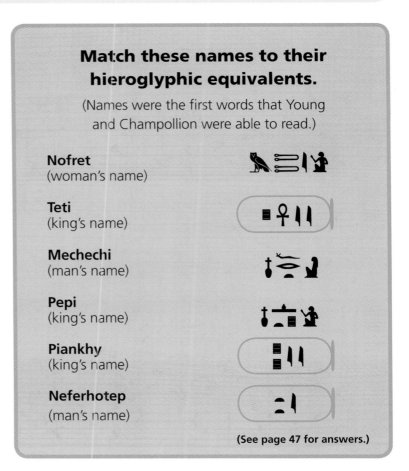

Match these names to their hieroglyphic equivalents.

(Names were the first words that Young and Champollion were able to read.)

Nofret (woman's name)

Teti (king's name)

Mechechi (man's name)

Pepi (king's name)

Piankhy (king's name)

Neferhotep (man's name)

(See page 47 for answers.)

Answers to Puzzles

Page 11

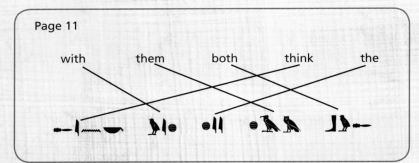

with   them   both   think   the

Page 14

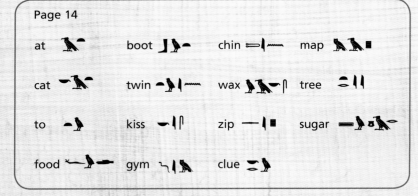

at   boot   chin   map

cat   twin   wax   tree

to   kiss   zip   sugar

food   gym   clue

Page 15

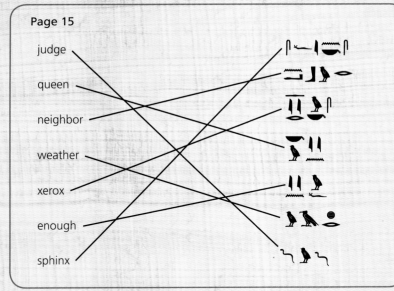

judge

queen

neighbor

weather

xerox

enough

sphinx

Page 19

= Patsy

= Tony

= Nancy

= Edward

= Joseph

= Christine

Page 21

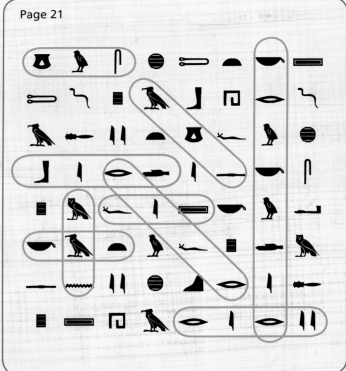

Page 26

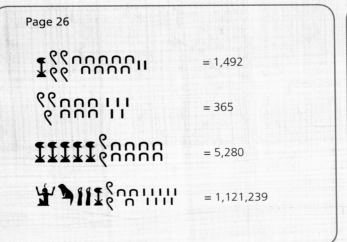

- = 1,492
- = 365
- = 5,280
- = 1,121,239

Page 27

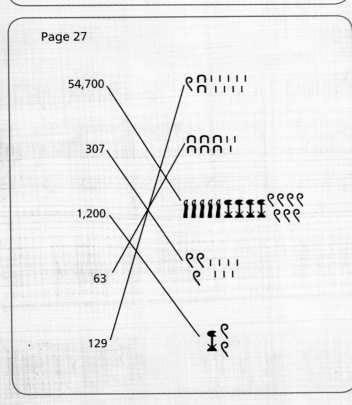

54,700

307

1,200

63

129

Page 30

1. = Mississippi (River)	13. = write or wrote
2. = Boston	14. = shine
3. = build	15. = whistle
4. = robin	16. = jog or jig
5. = Reuben or Robin	17. = lake
6. = Robin or Robyn	18. = look
7. = run	19. = trip
8. = Mark	20. = Moscow
9. = market	21. = many
10. = talk	22. = sing
11. = Washington (D.C.)	23. = New York
12. = Washington (George)	24. = Paris

Page 45

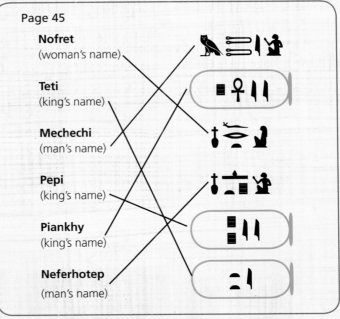

Nofret
(woman's name)

Teti
(king's name)

Mechechi
(man's name)

Pepi
(king's name)

Piankhy
(king's name)

Neferhotep
(man's name)

Credits

Except where noted, the works reproduced in this book are from the collection of The Metropolitan Museum of Art.

CASE

CASE COVER:
Coffin of Khnum-nakht (detail)
Egyptian (possibly Asyut), Dynasty 12 (ca. 1981–1802 BC)
Painted wood, L. 82 in.
Rogers Fund, 1915 15.2.2

Haremhab Before Isis (detail)
Egyptian (Thebes), Dynasty 18 (ca. 1323–1295 BC)
Copy of a wall painting from tomb of Haremhab;
tempera on paper, 13 x 24 ⅝ in.
Rogers Fund, 1923 23.2.85

CASE LINER:
Stela of Montuwoser (detail)
Egyptian, Dynasty 12 (ca. 1961–1917 BC)
Painted limestone, H. 41 1⁄16 in.
Gift of Edward S. Harkness, 1912 12.184

BOOK

BOOK COVER:
Coffin of Khnum-nakht (detail)
Egyptian (possibly Asyut), Dynasty 12 (ca. 1981–1802 BC)
Painted wood, L. 82 in.
Rogers Fund, 1915 15.2.2

Haremhab Before Isis (detail)
Egyptian (Thebes), Dynasty 18 (ca. 1323–1295 BC)
Copy of a wall painting from tomb of Haremhab;
tempera on paper, 13 x 24 ⅝ in.
Rogers Fund, 1923 23.2.85

TITLE PAGE:
Coffin of Khnum-nakht (detail)
Egyptian (possibly Asyut), Dynasty 12 (ca. 1981–1802 BC)
Painted wood, L. 82 in.
Rogers Fund, 1915 15.2.2

BORDERS:
Coffin of Khnum-nakht (detail)
Egyptian (possibly Asyut), Dynasty 12 (ca. 1981–1802 BC)
Painted wood, L. 82 in.
Rogers Fund, 1915 15.2.2

Journey to Abydos (detail)
Egyptian, Dynasty 18 (ca. 1550–1295 BC)
Copy of a wall painting from tomb of Pairy;
tempera on paper, 12 ¼ x 29 ½ in.
Rogers Fund, 1930 30.4.96

Inner Coffin of Khonsu (detail)
Egyptian (Thebes), Dynasty 19 (ca. 1279–1213 BC)
Painted wood and gesso, H. 74 in.
Funds from various donors, 1886 86.1.2a

Nofretari Kneeling in Adoration (detail)
Egyptian (Thebes), Dynasty 19 (ca. 1295–1186 BC)
Copy of a wall painting from tomb of Nofretari;
tempera on paper, 18 ⅛ x 13 ⅜ in.
Egyptian Expedition of The Metropolitan Museum of Art,
Rogers Fund, 1930 30.4.144

Stela of Aafenmut
Egyptian (Thebes), Dynasty 22 (ca. 924–889 BC)
Painted wood, H. 9 in.
Rogers Fund, 1928 28.3.35

Cat
Egyptian, Ptolemaic period (ca. 330–30 BC)
Bronze, H. 11 in.
Harris Brisbane Dick Fund, 1956 56.16.1

Sphinx of Amenhotep III
Egyptian, Dynasty 18 (ca. 1390–1352 BC)
Possibly from a model of a temple;
faience, remains of an alabaster tenon, L. 9 ⅞ in.
Purchase, Lila Acheson Wallace Gift, 1972 1972.125

Stela of Ptahmose (detail)
Egyptian, Dynasty 19 (ca. 1295–1186 BC)
Limestone, H. 56 in.
Harris Brisbane Dick Fund, 1967 67.3

Stela of the Chancellor Neferiu (detail)
Egyptian, Dynasty 9 (ca. 2100–2090 BC)
Painted limestone, H. 45 ½ in.
Gift of J. Pierpont Morgan, 1912 12.183.8

Haremhab Before Isis (detail)
Egyptian (Thebes), Dynasty 18 (ca. 1323–1295 BC)
Copy of a wall painting from tomb of Haremhab;
tempera on paper, 13 x 24 ⅝ in.
Rogers Fund, 1923 23.2.85

Menna and His Family Fishing and Fowling (detail)
Egyptian (Thebes), Dynasty 18 (ca. 1550–1295 BC)
Copy of a wall painting from tomb of Menna;
tempera on paper, 74 x 39 ½ in.
Rogers Fund, 1930 30.4.48

Prince and His Father, King Ramesses III, Before Hat-Hor
Egyptian (Thebes), Dynasty 20 (ca. 1195–1080 BC)
Copy of a wall painting from tomb of Amenkhepseshef;
tempera on paper, 37 ¼ x 25 ⅜ in.
Rogers Fund, 1933 33.8.7

The False Door of Mechechi (detail)
Egyptian, Dynasty 6 (ca. 2323–2150 BC)
Limestone, H. 55 ⅛ in.
Gift of Mr. and Mrs. J. J. Klejman, 1964 64.100

Stela of Montuwoser (detail)
Egyptian, Dynasty 12 (ca. 1961–1917 BC)
Painted limestone, H. 41 1⁄16 in.
Gift of Edward S. Harkness, 1912 12.184

Stela of Rehuerdjersen (detail)
Egyptian (Abydos), Dynasty 12 (ca. 1981–1952 BC)
Limestone, L. 18 ½ in.
Rogers Fund, 1912 12.182.1

Amenhotep III and His Mother, Mutemua, in a Kiosk
Egyptian (Thebes), Dynasty 18 (ca. 1390–1352 BC)
Copy of a wall painting from tomb 226;
tempera on paper, 89 x 63 ¾ in.
Rogers Fund, 1915 15.5.1

A Scribe (detail)
Egyptian (Thebes), Dynasty 18 (ca. 1550–1295 BC)
Copy of a wall painting from tomb of Menna;
tempera on paper, 29 ⅞ x 73 ¼ in.
Rogers Fund, 1930 30.4.44

The Vulture Goddess Nekhbet (detail)
Egyptian (Thebes), Dynasty 18 (ca. 1479–1458 BC)
Copy of a wall painting from shrine of Anubis, temple of Hatshepsut;
tempera on paper, 29 ½ x 41 ¾ in.
Rogers Fund, 1930 30.4.138

Amentet, Goddess of the West (detail)
Egyptian, Dynasty 25 (ca. 712–664 BC)
Panel from outer coffin of Pekherkhonsu;
painted wood, L. 22 in.
Rogers Fund, 1928 28.3.53

Coffin of Menqabu (detail)
Egyptian, First Intermediate Period (ca. 2100–2061 BC)
Painted wood, L. 76 ¾ in.
MUSEUM OF FINE ARTS, Boston
Emily Esther Sears Fund 03.1631a-b

Sacred Eye of Horus
Egyptian, Dynasty 18 (ca. 1390–1295 BC)
Faience, L. 3 ⅛ in.
Gift of Edward S. Harkness, 1926 26.7.1022

Coffin of Khnum-nakht
Egyptian (possibly Asyut), Dynasty 12 (ca. 1981–1802 BC)
Painted wood, L. 82 in.
Rogers Fund, 1915 15.2.2

Thoth (detail)
Egyptian (probably Meir), Roman period (ca. AD 60–70)
From a mummy mask; painted plaster and cartonnage, wig of flax, papyrus, and other plant fibers, H. 20 ⅞ in.
Rogers Fund, 1919 19.2.6

Scarab
Egyptian (Thebes), Dynasty 18 (ca. 1550–1295 BC)
Steatite, L. 3 ¾ in.
Rogers Fund, 1935 35.2.1

Horus Offering an Ankh (detail)
Egyptian (Lisht), Dynasty 12 (ca. 1981–1952 BC)
Limestone, L. 45 ½ in.
Rogers Fund 1908 08.200.6

Recording a Harvest (detail)
Egyptian (Thebes), Dynasty 18 (ca. 1550–1295 BC)
Copy of a wall painting from tomb of Menna;
tempera on paper, 29 ⅞ x 73 ¼ in.
Rogers Fund, 1930 30.4.44

Scribe's Palette and Brushes
Egyptian (Thebes), Dynasty 21 (ca. 1070–945 BC)
Wood, ink, and reed, L. 19 ⅛ in.
Harris Brisbane Dick Fund, 1947 47.123

Scribe Reading a Papyrus
Egyptian, Dynasty 18 (ca. 1550–1295 BC)
Serpentine and alabaster, H. 4 ⅞ in.
Anonymous Gift, 1931 31.4.1

Coffin of Khnum-nakht (detail)
Egyptian (possibly Asyut), Dynasty 12 (ca. 1981–1802 BC)
Painted wood, L. 82 in.
Rogers Fund, 1915 15.2.2

Artist's Gridded Sketch
Egyptian (Thebes), Dynasty 18 (ca. 1550–1295 BC)
Inked limestone, W. 5 ½ in.
Rogers Fund, 1923 23.3.4

Scribe's Writing Board
Egyptian (vicinity of Akhim), Dynasty 11 (ca. 2124–1981 BC)
Wood and gesso, H. 8 ⅝ in.
Gift of Edward S. Harkness, 1928 28.9.5

Nany's Funerary Papyri (detail)
Egyptian (Thebes), Dynasty 21 (ca. 1070–945 BC)
Inked papyrus, 14 ½ in. x 17 ft. 2 ½ in.
Excavations of The Metropolitan Museum of Art, 1929,
Rogers Fund, 1930 30.3.31

Outer Coffin of Nephthys (detail)
Egyptian, Dynasty 12 (ca. 1981–1802 BC)
Painted wood, L. 79 15⁄16 in.
Rogers Fund, 1911 11.150.15a

Letter for Heqa-nakht, Papyrus III
Egyptian (Thebes), Dynasty 12 (ca. 1981–1802 BC)
Papyrus, 10 ¼ x 5 ½ in.
Rogers Fund and Edward S. Harkness Gift, 1922
22.3.518 recto

Djehuty and His Mother Receiving Offerings (detail)
Egyptian (Thebes), Dynasty 18 (ca. 1427–1400 BC)
Copy of a wall painting from tomb of Djehuty;
tempera on paper, 17 5⁄16 x 19 5⁄16 in.
Rogers Fund, 1915 15.5.8

Rosetta Stone
Egyptian (el-Rashid), 196 BC
Basalt, H. 45 ½ in.
THE BRITISH MUSEUM, London

Relief of Nebhepetre Mentuhotep II (detail)
Egyptian (Thebes), Dynasty 11 (ca. 2051–2000 BC)
Painted limestone, 14 13⁄16 x 38 9⁄16 in.
Gift of Egypt Exploration Fund, 1907 07.230.2

Coptic Manuscript
Egyptian (Wadi an-Natrun), Coptic period (AD 200–1199)
Inked paper, H. 8 ⅞ in.
Rogers Fund, 1919 19.196.3